HARRIET TUBMAN

A Life From Beginning to End

Copyright © 2017 by Hourly History

All rights reserved.

Table of Contents

Introduction
Slavery in a new world
Araminta "Minty" Ross
Tubman, the freedom fighter
Civil War in the United States
Life after freedom
Lessons learned
Conclusion

Introduction

Slavery – it is defined in its simplest terms as the owning of one human being by another. It has been practiced by numerous cultures around the world throughout history, but nowhere has it left such deep, unhealed wounds as in the United States of America. The practice of owning slaves significantly profited US business ventures, particularly in the southern United States in the tobacco and cotton industries, by allowing them to minimize their labor costs which, in turn, helped to maximize profits. That, in turn, made it very difficult for those businesses to give up the practice, no matter how cruel or contradictory it was to the core values of the United States.

Slaves in the US were treated harshly, often worse than the way slave owners treated the animals they owned. They were regularly beaten, given only minimal housing and food, women were frequently raped, and all slaves were forced to work long hours (up to 15 hours per day) on labor-intensive tasks every day of the week except Sunday. The limitations of 15 hours per day and 6 days a week were only instituted after the Stono Rebellion, a slave rebellion in 1739 in South Carolina.

Practically speaking, slaves had no rights - not even the right to life. If they tried to escape, they were often executed in the most inhumane ways imaginable. Some slave owners allowed dogs to tear the runaway slave apart, while others cut the body into four quarters for public display. Decapitation and hanging were also common, and the bodies were left to decay in plain sight as a warning to others against trying to escape. If they weren't executed, their punishment for disobedience was usually equally as horrific. They could be whipped, mutilated, burned, shackled, castrated, and afterward, forced to wear a metal collar with spikes, which would embed into their neck as a reminder of their wrongdoing. Often after a whipping, overseers would order their wounds to be burst and rubbed with turpentine and red pepper. Punishments were regularly meted out for the slightest perceived infractions, including such behavior as walking too slowly and insubordination.

Slaves were also bound by laws that forbade them from leaving the plantation without a white person or a white person's permission, their homes were searched every two weeks for weapons or stolen goods, and they could not work for pay, plant certain crops such as corn, peas or rice, keep hogs, cattle, or horses, own or operate a boat, or buy, sell, or wear clothing finer than "Negro cloth." In some places, they were forbidden from learning to read, and more generally, the education of slaves was discouraged everywhere.

In short, the life of a slave was a living hell. It isn't surprising that many attempted to escape, even preferring death should they be caught, to remaining in captivity as a slave. The northern United States, though not free of prejudice and discrimination, had a more liberal attitude and eventually voted to abolish slavery within their borders in 1804. The emancipation of the northern slaves, however, proceeded gradually, such that it wasn't until after 1850 that the majority of slaves in these states had actually gained their freedom. Because of the more liberal attitude in these northern states, they became destinations for runaway slaves from the south, even before they voted to abolish slavery.

In approximately 1780, a network of safe houses, escape routes, and conductors were established running from the south to the northern states. By the 1830s, it was known as the Underground Railroad, and the homes and businesses that harbored runaways were known as stations or depots. They were run by stationmasters; conductors were people who moved the fugitives from one station to the next. One of the most famous conductors in the Underground Railroad was Harriet Tubman. A runaway slave herself, Tubman risked being recaptured to return to slave states 19 times and is credited with bringing more than 300 slaves to freedom.

Harriet Tubman was born Araminta "Minty" Ross in Maryland. Historians differ as to the exact year of her birth, but a midwife payment and other historical documents, including an advertisement regarding her status as a runaway, strongly suggest she was born in 1822. Tubman, herself, claimed her date of birth variously as 1820, 1822, and 1825, indicating she likely was not sure of her birth year. Her parents were Harriet "Rit" Green and Ben Ross, and they were owned by different slaveholders, something which resulted in their family being torn apart. Tubman's grandmother, Modesty, was brought to the United States on a slave ship, and Tubman was told as a child she was of Ashanti lineage, but there is no evidence to either confirm or deny this assertion, and there is no information about any of her other ancestors.

Minty married John Tubman, a free black man, in 1844, and soon after changed her name from Araminta to Harriet. It is not clear why she changed her name, but it may have been related to a religious conversion or in honor of a relative, perhaps her mother. Some scholars suggest she changed it right after the wedding, but others argue it was closer to her planned escape in 1849. Blended marriages between free blacks and slaves were common in the eastern part of Maryland since, by this time, half the black population there was free. The law dictated, however, that because the mother was enslaved, any children born to the couple would be enslaved as well.

After the death of Tubman's slave owner, Edward Brodess, his widow began the process of trying to sell the family's slaves. As a child, Tubman had witnessed her birth family torn apart because they were owned by different slaveholders, and she had no desire to see the same thing happen with her conjugal family. Thus, she began to plan her escape, later recalling, "There was one of two things I had a right to – liberty or death. If I could not have one, I would have the other." (Bradford 1961, p. 29)

Tubman initially escaped with her two brothers, Ben and Henry, but after leaving, the brothers had second thoughts and went back. Harriet was forced to return with them, but she escaped again soon after that, this time without them. The experience of having to turn back with her brothers may have been the reason behind why later, as a conductor, she reportedly carried a gun and threatened to shoot runaways without a second thought.

After securing freedom for herself, she then began courageous efforts to rescue friends and family members. Because of her efforts, William Lloyd Garrison nicknamed her Moses, after the Biblical prophet who led the Hebrew slaves to freedom from Egypt. Tubman was first prompted to return to Maryland when she learned her two children, James Alfred and Araminta, were about to be sold along with her niece, Kessiah. Kessiah was married to a free black man who made the winning bid for her in the auction. After doing so, he and Kessiah escaped with the two children when the auctioneer went to lunch. That night, they met with Tubman in Baltimore, where she then led them to freedom in Philadelphia. After that, Tubman began making regular trips to guide more family members and friends to freedom.

Over the course of the next 11 years, Harriet Tubman would make thirteen expeditions and personally free more than 70 slaves, including her brothers, their wives, and some of their children. She also provided instructions to a number of other runaways who were then able to escape successfully. She took various precautions, including working in the winter when people stayed inside at night, and leaving on a Saturday night since the newspapers wouldn't publish runaway notices until Monday morning. She also disguised herself and would use props, such as live chickens, to give the impression she was running errands. In fact, she once used the chickens, whom she agitated so they would make noise, as a distraction so a former owner who was walking toward her would not make eye contact. On another occasion, she pretended to read upon seeing a former master, who ignored her as a result since it was known Tubman was illiterate.

Harriet Tubman was never captured, nor was any of the fugitives she led to freedom. One of her last missions was to free her aging parents, whom she guided to Ontario, Canada where former slaves, including Tubman's brothers, had formed a community. Tubman also assisted the northern forces during the Civil War, and in her later years promoted the cause of women's suffrage, working alongside such notable suffragists as Susan B. Anthony and Emily Howland.

Tubman embodied the words found in the Pledge of Allegiance for the United States of America, "...with liberty and justice for all." Her courage in the face of such hate-filled oppression remains a relevant example for freedom seekers around the world today, and her refusal to allow oppression to dominate her life should stand as a symbol of human dedication, selflessness, and perseverance through difficult times. Her life is a timeless illustration of what Martin Luther King, Jr. meant when he said, "Human progress is neither automatic nor inevitable...Every step toward the goal of justice requires sacrifice, suffering, and struggle; the tireless exertions and passionate concern of dedicated individuals." There has been a no more dedicated, passionate individual to the cause of equality than Harriet Tubman.

Chapter One

Slavery in a new world

"My people have a country of their own to go to if they choose... Africa... but, this America belongs to them just as much as it does to any of the white race... in some ways even more so, because they gave the sweat of their brow and their blood in slavery so that many parts of America could become prosperous and recognized in the world."

—Josephine Baker

Slavery in the United States began in 1619 when the first African slaves were brought to Jamestown, Virginia by Dutch traders. The early settlements in America had difficulty attracting and retaining laborers because of the harsh frontier conditions, and thus, both indentured servitude and slavery offered solutions. Indentured servants were not slaves, but were required to work for between four and seven years in order to work off the cost of their passage and maintenance. Some historians estimate that over one-half of the early *white* immigrants to the North American colonies came as indentured servants.

Because the early African slaves were typically baptized by the Spanish before leaving Africa, they were also treated as indentured servants since English law exempted Christians from slavery. In this way, many Africans belonging to what is often referred to as the charter generation in the colonies earned their freedom after working the prescribed period of time and were subsequently given the use of land and supplies from their former masters. During this period, there were no laws regarding slavery, but in 1640, an African indentured servant named John Punch was sentenced by a Virginia court to lifelong slavery for attempting to flee his servitude. The two white men who fled with him received only an additional year of servitude as their punishment. The case represented the first legal sanctioning of slavery and set an official precedent distinguishing Europeans from Africans.

Shortly thereafter, in 1641, Massachusetts became the first colony to legally authorize slavery by passing the Body of Liberties. The law prohibited slavery in many cases, but it did allow for three legal basis for slavery. The act stated that slaves could be held in the following circumstances: 1) if they were captured in war; 2) if they sold themselves into slavery or were purchased from elsewhere and; 3) if they were sentenced to slavery as punishment. The Body of Liberties used the word "strangers" as slaves, and the term came to be synonymous with Native Americans and Africans.

During the colonial period, laws regarding slavery were gradually refined since the practice existed in all of the colonies. In the southern colonies, a growing agricultural economy dependent on commodity crops, most notably tobacco, rice, and indigo, became heavily dependent on the use of slave labor. By 1720, approximately 65% of the people in South Carolina consisted of slaves. It wasn't until after the American Revolution that cotton became a major crop in the area. The invention of the cotton gin in 1793 enabled the cultivation of cotton in a variety of areas. As with other commodity crops, cotton agriculture also relied mainly on slave labor. Thus, the flourishing economy of the southern United States was able to maximize profits quite literally on the backs of African slaves.

Between the colonial period and 1860, it is estimated some 12 million slaves were brought to the Americas from Africa. The majority were transported to sugar colonies in the Caribbean and Brazil, where life expectancy was much shorter than in the US; the slave population, therefore, required constant replenishment. In the US, the slave population had reached 4 million by the time of the 1860 census, with the growth of enslaved people being far greater than the population of any European nation and nearly twice that of England.

Following the American Revolution, the Constitution of the United States, which took effect in 1789, contained several provisions regarding slavery, one of which established that slaves would be counted as three-fifths of a person for purposes of calculating state populations. Because of the number of slaves in the southern states, this rule strengthened the political power of their representatives. Additionally, between the election of George Washington, the first US president, and Abraham Lincoln, the 16th, no president was elected to a second term who was not a slaveholder. The result was that the southern states dominated both the Congress and the American presidency for nearly 50 years.

Despite the influence of the southern delegations in the post-Revolutionary War era, abolition movements, buoyed by the young country's ideology of freedom for all, resulted in the abolition of slavery in every northern state, with the last being New Jersey in 1804. No southern state, however, abolished slavery. Tensions began to build between the progressive abolitionists that dominated the north and the southerners who profited greatly from slave labor. Slaveholders began to refer to slavery as the "peculiar institution," and justified it by claiming it was less cruel than the free labor of the north.

It was in this environment of increasing tension between the northern and southern states that a network of safe houses was established to harbor runaway slaves and guide them to safety in the north. It was known as the Underground Railroad, and the houses and businesses that harbored runaways were known as stations or depots. The owners of the stations were called stationmasters, and the guides who escorted the fugitives were known as conductors. According to one estimate, the Underground Railroad assisted 100,000 runaways to escape from the south successfully.

Because of the political power wielded by the southern states, the north was obliged to assist in the recapture of runaway slaves. It required very little documentation to prove that someone was a slave, and as a result, many free blacks were unjustly captured and sold into slavery. Those captured had little legal recourse to prove their free status, and in those cases brought before judges, the judges were paid more if they ruled the individual was a slave than if they ruled he or she was a free black. Thus, the system heavily favored the slaveholders, who exaggerated the number of escapees. As a result, many northern states ignored the Fugitive Slave Act of 1793 that required them to assist with the recapture of runaway slaves. This was cited by the southern states as a major reason for their secession from the union, which led to the American Civil War.

The American Civil War began in April of 1861 under President Abraham Lincoln, and it ended with the collapse of the Confederate (southern) government in the spring of 1865. During the four years of intense fighting, between 620,000 and 750,000 soldiers died, a number higher than American deaths in World War I and World War II combined. President Lincoln, himself, became a victim of the war when he was assassinated on April 14, 1865, by John Wilkes Booth. Moreover, the divisions created by the war often resulted in brothers fighting brothers, and it left a deep wound in the United States that has yet to heal fully. In the end, slavery was abolished nationwide, the union was maintained, and over the years, the descendants of the Africans brought to the US as slaves have fought, and continue to fight, tirelessly for their civil rights. While much has been accomplished toward that end, much remains to be done.

There were many heroes who emerged during the struggle for freedom from slavery in the United States and the subsequent fight for equality. One who stands out among those was a small woman, about five feet tall, who had suffered a head injury that left her with a type of epilepsy, one of the symptoms of which is narcolepsy—the tendency to fall asleep at any given moment. She was born Araminta Ross, but she is best-known to the world as Harriet Tubman. She was single-handedly responsible for bringing hundreds of runaway slaves to freedom, and she, along with the other committed, tireless freedom fighters along the Underground Railroad, changed the world. Their courage in the face of the dangers they confronted on a regular basis stands as a shining example for the world to follow in difficult times. Indeed, they offer us living proof of anthropologist Margaret Mead's assertion when she stated, "Never doubt that a small group of thoughtful, committed citizens can change the world; indeed, it's the only thing that ever has."

Chapter Two

Araminta "Minty" Ross

"Some are born great, some achieve greatness, and some have greatness thrust upon them."

—William Shakespeare

Araminta "Minty" Ross was born to Harriet "Rit" Green and Ben Ross most likely sometime in the early 1820s. Tubman, herself, variously cited her birth year as 1820, 1822, and 1825, suggesting even she didn't know the actual year. A receipt for payment to a midwife, along with various other documents including her runaway slave notice, strongly support the contention that the year of her birth was 1822.

There is only scant information about Tubman's family. Her grandmother, Modesty, was brought to the United States on a slave ship from Africa. Tubman was told she was of Ashanti lineage—a native group in the Ashanti Region of modern day Ghana. Her mother, Rit, may have had a white father and was a cook for the Pattison Brodess family. Her father, Ben, was a woodsman who worked on the Anthony Thompson plantation.

Her parents had a total of nine children, and they struggled to keep the family together. Since they were owned by different slaveholders, however, the children were considered the property of the mother's owner, Edward Brodess, who sold three of the daughters (Linah, Mariah Ritty, and Soph) thereby separating the family forever. When a trader wanted to buy another child, Moses, who was Rit's youngest son, Rit hid him for a month. She subsequently threatened Brodess and the interested buyer when they eventually came to seize her son, reportedly saying, "…the first man that comes into my house, I will split his head open." (Larson 2004, p. 33) Incredibly, Brodess and the buyer backed off. The stories told to Tubman about this event had a powerful impact on her beliefs regarding the possibility of resistance.

Tubman, as was typical of many families in that day, spent much of her childhood taking care of her younger brother and an infant sibling. Because of her experience as a nursemaid, Brodess hired her out as such to a woman named "Miss Susan." She was tasked with watching Miss Susan's baby as it slept and she was harshly punished if the child cried. On one occasion, she was whipped so badly that it left scars she carried for the rest of her life. It was at this time that Tubman began to resist her overseers. She would run away for a few days, wear several layers of clothing to protect against the beatings, and even fight back physically.

Later on, Tubman was hired out to another family as an adolescent, and it was on one occasion during this time that she was sent to a store for supplies. While there, she ran into a slave owned by another family who had left the fields where he worked without permission. His overseer had found him and furiously asked Tubman to help restrain him, but she refused, and the slave ran away. The overseer attempted to stop him by throwing a two-pound weight at him, but the weight struck Tubman in the head instead. She later joked about the incident saying that her unruly hair, which had never been combed and stood out on top of her head, had saved her life. She suffered a serious head injury, however, and remained unconscious for two days without any medical care. Upon waking, she was sent back into the fields. The injury resulted in lifelong problems with apparent seizures. She would seemingly fall asleep, though she claimed to be fully aware of her surroundings during these attacks. Some medical experts suggest she may have suffered from temporal lobe epilepsy, which can create such symptoms.

Following her head injury, Tubman also experienced powerful visions and dreams throughout her life. She interpreted these as revelations from God. She was illiterate as a child, but she had been told Bible stories by her mother, and she developed a passionate faith in God as a result. However, she rejected the teachings in the New Testament that called for slaves to be obedient and instead found inspiration in the tales of deliverance related in various books of the Old Testament. Though she remained devoutly faithful throughout her life, the particular branch of her Christian faith remains unclear.

As a young adult, Araminta married a free black man named John Tubman in 1844, but little is known about him beyond his status as a free man. Blended marriages between enslaved people and free people were common during this time in Maryland. There was a large African-

American population there, and the policies treating African slaves as indentured servants had resulted in a substantial number of slaves, approximately 50% of the black population in the region at the time, who had fulfilled their time as servants and subsequently gained their freedom. Many of these blended marriages would result in the free partner buying the freedom of the enslaved spouse, and some have suggested that might have been the plan with Tubman. After her marriage, Tubman changed her name to Harriet, possibly to honor a relative and possibly as part of a religious conversion. The timing of the change is subject to debate, with some scholars saying it occurred right after her marriage but others saying it was closer to her planned escape in 1849, and might have been part of a plan to assist her in that regard.

In 1849, Tubman made her first attempt at escape. The attempt was made on September 17, and for Tubman, it was in response to the Brodess family's attempts to sell her. First, Edward Brodess tried to sell her after she became ill, and then after he died shortly thereafter, his widow began to sell off the family's slaves. Interestingly, Tubman later said that she prayed that Edward Brodess would change his mind about selling her, and when it became apparent that wasn't going to happen, she prayed for his death. A week later he was dead. Notably, despite the bad treatment she endured under his ownership, Tubman expressed regret for her prayer. Once his widow renewed the efforts to sell Tubman, however, she made the decision to escape.

On September 17, 1849, Tubman ran away with her two brothers, Ben and Harry. At the time, Tubman had been hired out to Dr. Anthony Thompson, whose plantation was in an area called Poplar Neck in Caroline County, Maryland. Most scholars believe her brothers had been hired out to work on that plantation as well. It was an opportune time for the escape attempt because, since they were on loan to the Thompson plantation, their owner, Eliza Brodess, didn't realize they were gone for another two weeks when she finally posted a runaway notice offering 100 dollars for the return of all three slaves. There were complicating factors for Tubman's brothers, however, including the possibility that Ben had just become a father. The two brothers made the decision to return; Tubman was forced to go with them.

Shortly after the failed escape attempt, Tubman made with her brothers; she made another attempt alone. Before leaving, she sent a farewell message to her mother in the form of a coded song that a trusted friend of hers sang to her. The words said, in part, "I'll meet you in the morning. I'm bound for the promised land." Tubman used the Underground Railroad to make her escape, but the exact route remains unknown. It is likely that she made use of stations in the Poplar Neck area owned by Quakers, whose beliefs prohibited slavery. A common route from that area included going northeast along the Choptank River through Delaware and then from there into Pennsylvania. It was some 90 miles (145 kilometers) from Poplar Neck to freedom, but the journey, which would have been undertaken on foot, likely took between five days and three weeks. Tubman traveled at night, using the North Star as a guide, and as part of deception employed at an early stop was forced to sweep the yard of the house so as to appear to be working for the family. When she finally arrived in Pennsylvania, she was filled with awe and relief. She stated, among other things, that, "There was such a glory over everything; the sun came like gold through the trees, and over the fields, and I felt like I was in Heaven." (Bradford 1971, p. 19)

After gaining her freedom, Tubman realized that, despite the relief and happiness she felt, she was alone in this new land. She also soon learned that her children would be sold at an upcoming auction. That, along with rising tensions in a new country conflicted by the discrepancy between its moral ideals and the brutal realities of slavery, prompted Tubman to make the decision to work to free other slaves - starting with her own children. In essence, the realities of life for slaves in the United States of America were in the process of thrusting greatness upon this determined young woman!

Chapter Three

Tubman, the freedom fighter

"Every great dream begins with a dreamer. Always remember, you have within you the strength, the patience, and the passion to reach for the stars to change the world."

—Harriet Tubman

Harriet Tubman certainly rose to the occasion as she found herself in the midst of growing turmoil in a young country struggling with high ideals pitted against cruel realities. Tubman risked her life to return to slave country on 19 different expeditions in order to bring slaves to freedom. She used ingenious methods to conduct her passengers safely, and neither she nor any of the fugitives she assisted were ever caught.

After rescuing her children and niece in December of 1850, Tubman returned the following spring to Maryland to assist her brother Moses and two other unidentified men with their escape. At that time, she was likely working with a Quaker in Delaware named Thomas Garrett. She was successful in guiding these three men to safety, and with each subsequent trip, she gained more confidence.

Her methods involved working at night and during the winter when most people would be in their homes, and leaving on a Saturday so that Monday would be the earliest that a runaway slave notice could be placed in the newspaper. Additionally, while making the escape with her fugitives, she would sing to them in codes to telegraph the safety, or lack thereof, of moving forward. She would change the tempo of the song "Go Down Moses" to indicate whether or not it was safe to proceed. There were no common codes used by Underground Railroad conductors, but "Go Down Moses" was a song that the black regiments would sing later in the Civil War.

Tubman had other methods, of course, including various distraction techniques, such as using chickens to keep people from making eye contact with her and appearing to read so that onlookers would not suspect she was who she was since it was known she was illiterate. Additionally, Tubman worked with a network of notable abolitionists including Thomas Garrett, Sam Green, William and Nat Brinkley, Abraham Gibbs, William Still, and perhaps most notably, Frederick Douglass. Garrett was a Quaker dedicated to the abolitionist movement, the Brinkleys and Gibbs were free black agents along the Underground Railroad route, and William Still was a famous black agent who has since been credited with helping hundreds of runaway slaves reach New York, New England, and southern Ontario in Canada.

Frederick Douglass was an escaped slave himself from Maryland who became a famous social reformer, orator, abolitionist, writer, and eventually a statesman. He was the national leader of the abolitionist movement in New York and Massachusetts and was famous for his engaging lectures and insightful antislavery writings. Slaveholders had argued that Africans lacked the intellectual capacity to be independent citizens, and Douglass provided northern abolitionists with proof that was not true. Along with his many impressive accomplishments, which include writing several autobiographical books, traveling nationally and internationally to give lectures, and becoming President of the Freedman's Savings Bank, he also accepted an appointment as United States Marshal for the District of Columbia when President Rutherford B. Hayes offered him the position in 1874. He also became the first black man to receive a vote for President of the United States at the 1888 Republican National Convention.

Of course, Douglass also worked on the Underground Railroad, harboring runaway slaves and helping to get them to safety in the north. It was there that he likely worked with Tubman in December of 1851 when she guided 11 fugitives northward. Douglass wrote of harboring 11 fugitives under his roof, noting it was the largest group he had ever taken in. Additionally, he worked to collect sufficient money to get them to Canada, sheltering and feeding them until he had collected enough. The number of fugitives mentioned and the timing makes it likely these 11 freedom seekers were Tubman's group. They certainly admired one another as evidenced by the fact that Tubman asked him for a letter of commendation when one of her early biographies was being prepared in 1868. He wrote back to her, saying in part, "I need such words from you far more than you can need them from me, especially where your superior labors and devotion to the cause of the lately enslaved of our land are known as I know them." (Bradford 1961, pp. 134–135)

Tubman's routes along the Underground Railroad included stations in East New Market and Poplar Neck, Maryland, Sandtown, Willow Grove, and the Camden area in Delaware as well as Dover, Smyrna, Blackbird, Chesapeake, New Castle, and Wilmington. At one point, she also returned to Dorchester County, Maryland to find her husband, John. He had, however, in her absence married another woman named Caroline. Tubman had purchased a suit for him after working various jobs earning money to pay for it. She was so upset that upon learning that he refused to join her in the north, she planned to make a scene at their house. But she subsequently decided that he was not worth the effort and focused her attention on helping slaves in need instead. For his part, John remained with his new wife, and they raised a family together. They lived happily for 16 years before he was killed during an argument with a white man named Robert Vincent.

Tubman's religious faith also played a large role in her life as a freedom fighter. Her head injury left her with visions and vivid dreams, which she interpreted as divine premonitions. Thomas Garrett wrote about her visions, noting that he had never met another person of color who had more confidence that God was speaking directly to her soul. She often used spirituals as coded messages to signal her passengers on the Railroad of danger or to indicate a clear path. She didn't just rely on her religion, however, as she is also known to have carried a revolver, and to have used it as protection and to threaten any escaped slave who attempted to turn back. One story purports that she pointed her revolver at the head of a reticent slave and told him, "You go on or die." (Conrad 1942, p. 14)

While Tubman's successes in aiding runaway slaves were noted by slaveholders, her identity was never known to them. There is no evidence to support a legend that a $40,000 reward was offered for her, and there is significant evidence to support the contention the story is untrue. Instead, slaveholders who were dismayed by the numerous escapes in their communities had begun to suspect a northern, white abolitionist, John Brown, of coming to the area to lure slaves away. Brown was later tried for treason against the state of Virginia and hanged after an unsuccessful raid on an arsenal in Harper's Ferry, an incident in 1859 which is widely considered a catalyst for the American Civil War. Thus, it appears Tubman was never on the slaveholder's radar. She was never captured, nor were any of the fugitives she assisted. She rightfully claimed, "I never ran my train off the track and I never lost a passenger." (Clinton, p. 192)

While John Brown was not the person the slaveholders were looking for, he did work with Harriet Tubman. She met him in April of 1858 and began helping him prepare for the attack on slaveholders at Harper's Ferry. Her knowledge of support networks was useful for his planning purposes, and she helped him recruit former slaves willing to participate in the raid. She was so useful, Brown referred to her as General Tubman. The initial date of the raid had to be postponed, however, and when it was rescheduled, Tubman could not be contacted to participate. Scholars debate the reasons why, with some saying she was ill and others saying that she 1was in various other locations recruiting more former slaves for the raid. Still others suggest she may have begun to believe, as Frederick Douglass did, that the raid was not a viable plan. As it turned out, it wasn't, and as fortune would have it, Tubman was not there. She later praised Brown effusively, stating that he had done more by dying than another 100 men could do by living, for it was his actions that served as a catalyst for the eventual liberation of all slaves after the Civil War.

In 1859, Tubman was able to acquire a small piece of land from Republican US Senator William H. Seward on the outskirts of Auburn, New York. It was in an area of antislavery activism, and it was then that Tubman made the decision to bring her parents to the property from the community established by escaped slaves, including her brothers, in Ontario, Canada. She did so in order that they should not have to suffer the harsh Canadian winters. Her siblings objected to the decision since they worried about the possibility that they could be caught and returned to the south in accordance with the Fugitive Slave Act. The antislavery activity in the area, however, seemed to assuage any fears Tubman might have had about that, and she used the property for years to take in relatives and boarders, many of which were black Americans seeking a better life.

After acquiring the property, Tubman returned again to Maryland to rescue a girl she referred to as her niece. The girl was 8-years-old, very light-skinned, and her name was Margaret. This particular expedition is shrouded in mystery because there is a question about the girl's real identity. Specifically, her parents were apparently free blacks, and the girl had been residing in a loving home with her twin brother. Indeed, the girl's daughter, years later, would call Tubman's action selfish since she had taken the girl from a sheltered home with loving family members to a place where there was no one to take care of her, and she also referred it as a kidnapping.

These events have caused some scholars to argue that Margaret was Tubman's own daughter. The two had a strong bond and even Margaret's daughter Alice admits there was a strong resemblance between the two. There is no concrete evidence that this was the case, but Tubman knew the pain of being separated from her mother, and given her strong moral base, it is unlikely she would intentionally cause the separation of a free family. However, it remains an open question.

Tubman's last expedition was in November of 1860 when she attempted to secure the release of her sister Rachel's children, Ben and Angerine. She had also intended to free her sister, but upon arriving in Maryland, she learned that her sister had died. She needed a $30 bribe to rescue the children, but she had no money, and they remained enslaved as a result. It is not known what happened to them. Tubman didn't waste the trip, however, as she found another group who were ready and willing to make the trip north, and while the trip took longer than expected, they arrived safely in New York on December 28, 1860.

In honor of all of the courageous efforts undertaken by Tubman to free African-Americans from slavery, noted abolitionist William Lloyd Garrison named her Moses after the Biblical prophet who led the Hebrews to freedom from their Egyptian slaveholders. The comparison is indeed relevant. The end of Tubman's expeditions did not mark the end of her activism. She continued to work for an end to slavery by assisting the northern forces during the Civil War and later fighting for women's equality.

Chapter Four
Civil War in the United States

"This is a world of compensations; and he who would be no slave, must consent to have no slave."

—Abraham Lincoln, in an 1859 letter to Henry Pierce

Harriet Tubman played a significant role in the American Civil War. The war broke out in 1861, and, seeing it as the key to the abolition of slavery in the United States, Tubman immediately began to help the war effort. She began working in the camps at Port Royal, South Carolina. There, she assisted fugitives, serving as a nurse rendering assistance to soldiers suffering from dysentery and small pox. She also met with General David Hunter, who was a strong supporter of abolition. After their meeting, Hunter declared the fugitives in Port Royal who had been designated as contraband, that is, property seized by northern forces, to be free. President Lincoln, however, was not yet ready to enforce emancipation and reprimanded Hunter. Tubman condemned the response, stating that God would not allow a victory over the south until Lincoln did the right thing.

Lincoln did do the right thing in January of 1863 when he issued the Emancipation Proclamation, declaring more than 3 million enslaved people in the south to be free. The immediate effect was that as soon as slaves escaped the control of the Confederate government, they became legally free, but eventually, it liberated all designated slaves. Tubman renewed her support for the defeat of the Confederacy and began leading bands of scouts through the land around Port Royal. She mapped the unfamiliar terrain of the area and documented the inhabitants. She also provided intelligence to Colonel James Montgomery that assisted him with the capture of Jacksonville, Florida.

Later in 1863, Tubman became the first woman to lead an armed assault in the Civil War. The assault was on a collection of plantations along the Combahee River in South Carolina. Tubman advised Montgomery and accompanied him on the raid. On June 2, 1863, she guided steamboats around mines in the river to reach the shore, and once there, the Union troops set fire to the plantations, destroyed their infrastructure, and seized food and supplies worth thousands of dollars. More than 750 slaves were rescued in the raid that day. Tubman was praised for her efforts, and most of the newly liberated men joined the Union army.

During the next two years, Tubman continued to assist the Union army by scouting into Confederate territory, nursing soldiers, and tending to newly liberated slaves. Upon the surrender of the Confederacy in 1865, she worked for several more months and then headed home. Despite her honorable service during the war, while on the train home, she was forcibly expelled into the smoking car, and suffered a broken arm from the manhandling. Several white passengers cursed her and demanded that she be kicked off the train. The government was also slow in recognizing her for her war effort. She had never received a constant salary, and after the war was denied compensation for years. Because of her unofficial status, she was denied a pension until 1899. This caused her great hardship as she continued her humanitarian efforts, which kept her in constant poverty.

    It is clear that, despite the army's failure to recognize her efforts, Tubman provided invaluable assistance to the Union effort. Her contributions provided valuable intelligence and insight that had immediate effects, enabling victories by Union forces. Her dedication and perseverance through such a difficult time in United States history is a testament to her character. Harriet Tubman is a true American war hero, and deserves recognition as such!

Chapter Five
Life after freedom

"I slept and dreamt that life was joy. I awoke and saw that life was service. I acted and behold, service was joy."

—Rabindranath Tagore

Tubman continued to dedicate her life to the service of others after the war ended. She supported her elderly parents and helped other people in need. She took in boarders to help pay the bills. She took in a Civil War veteran named Nelson Davis, who worked as a bricklayer in Auburn. They fell in love, and despite the fact that she was 22 years older than him, they married on March 18, 1869. They were together for the next 20 years and adopted a baby girl named Gertie.

Tubman's friends and growing number of admirers worked to support her, raising funds through various means. Sarah Hopkins Bradford was one admirer who wrote two biographers to help support Tubman's humanitarian efforts. These did bring in over $1000 to support Tubman, but unfortunately, she later fell prey to a scam involving a gold transfer. Two men claimed to be in possession of a cache of gold they said they smuggled out of South Carolina, Tubman knew that many southerners did bury valuables to hide them from Union forces and that black men were often assigned to digging details so it would be possible they could have found a cache of valuables. Given her financial woes and good nature, she was a prime victim and took the men in. They wanted to sell the gold to her for $2000, claiming it was worth $5000. Once they had lured her into the woods to collect the treasure, however, they attacked her, stole her purse, and bound and gagged her. New York responded with outrage, with most sympathizing with her hardships and lambasting the con men. Two Representatives, Clinton D. MacDougall of New York and Gerry W. Hazelton of Wisconsin, even introduced a bill to pay Tubman $2000 for her services during the Civil War, but the bill was defeated.

Despite the many setbacks she suffered, Tubman continued to work tirelessly in the service of others. After being asked by a white woman if she believed that women should have the right to vote, Tubman responded that she had suffered enough to believe it. She then began attending meetings at suffragist organizations and was soon speaking in favor of women's equality. She worked with such notable suffragists as Susan B. Anthony and Emily Howland. She gave a number of speeches detailing her activities during the Civil War, which certainly bolstered her assertion of equality. Her activism kindled a new wave of admiration for her achievements, and soon she was being profiled as part of a series on eminent women by a publication called *The Woman's Era*. As a result, a number of receptions were held in Boston honoring Tubman and her life's work. In typical fashion, her contributions to others had left her lacking the money to buy train tickets to these celebrations, and she had to sell a cow in order to attend.

At the turn of the 20th century, Tubman donated a parcel of land to the African Methodist Episcopal Zion Church with instructions that it be made into a home for aged, indigent "colored people." While the home was eventually opened, the church wanted to charge incoming residents $100. Tubman said that she wanted the rule to say that no one would be admitted unless they didn't have any money at all. Despite her frustration with the rule, she did attend the opening as the guest of honor on June 23, 1908. The home was called the Harriet Tubman Home for the Aged.

As for her health, Tubman continued to suffer the seizures, headaches, and other consequences of her childhood trauma. In the late 1890s, she underwent brain surgery at Massachusetts General Hospital in Boston. She stated the doctor had raised up her skull and it felt considerably more comfortable after the operation. Rather than receive anesthesia, she chose to bite down on a bullet as she had seen in the Civil War when soldiers had their limbs amputated.

By 1911, frail, ill, and penniless, she was admitted to the home named in her honor. A report on it in a New York newspaper prompted a new round of donations. In 1913, surrounded by friends and family members, Harriet Tubman died of pneumonia. Her last words were, "I go to prepare a place for you." She was buried at the Fort Hill Cemetery in Auburn with semi-military honors. Her tombstone was purchased by the Empire State Federation of Women's Clubs and was not erected until 1937. Her name is engraved on the front of the stone, and on the back, there is an inscription commemorating her work with the Underground Railroad and her role in the Civil War. Her faith is represented with the inscription, "Servant of God, Well Done." Hers was, in fact, a life well-done.

Chapter Six

Lessons learned

"Born lowly, she lived a life of exalted self – sacrifice and her end closes a career that has taken its place in American history. Her true services to the black race were never known but her true worth could never have been rewarded by human agency."

—Harriet Tubman Obituary article in the Auburn Citizen, Tuesday, March 11, 1913

The legacy of Harriet Tubman's life continues to this day. She inspired generations of African-Americans as they continue to struggle for equality in the United States. Dozens of schools are named in her honor, her home in Auburn is now a monument, as is the Harriet Tubman Museum in Cambridge. In 1944, the *SS Harriet Tubman* was launched as the first Liberty ship ever named for a black woman. In 1978, the United State Postal Service issued a stamp in her honor. President Barack Obama signed a proclamation creating the Harriet Tubman Underground Railroad National Monument on the Eastern Shore of Maryland in 2013. She has been included on a list of the 100 greatest African-Americans, there are two statues of her, one in Manhattan and one at Salisbury University, and in 2014, an asteroid was named in her honor. She has been declared a National Historic Person, and in 2016, the US Treasury Secretary announced plans to add her to the front of the twenty-dollar bill, relegating President Andrew Jackson, a slave owner, to the rear of the bill.

Her most important legacy, however, has to be the inspiration she has provided to African-Americans who looked to her example of courage in the face of death as they have struggled and continue to struggle, for equality. In fact, she is an inspiration to all Americans who struggle for their rights, regardless of race. Her perseverance in the face of the most extreme oppression and a lifetime of poverty is the definition of service and individual sacrifice. Oprah Winfrey said of her, "I have crossed over on the backs of Sojourner Truth, Harriet Tubman, Fannie Lou Hamer, and Madam C.J. Walker. Because of them, I can now live the dream. I am the seed of the free and I know it. I intend to bear great fruit."

Her efforts, and those of countless other abolitionists, freedom fighters, and equality advocates, bore great fruit in the years after the Civil War. In 1867, Congress passed a series of Reconstruction acts that guaranteed the civil rights of freed slaves. In 1868, the Fourteenth Amendment to the United States Constitution was ratified. It defined citizenship to include those born as slaves, thereby nullifying the Dred Scott case of 1857, which had ruled that blacks were not citizens. In 1870, the Fifteenth Amendment to the Constitution gave blacks the right to vote. In 1909, the National Association for the Advancement of Coloured People was founded and is still actively fighting for civil rights today. In 1920, the Nineteenth Amendment to the US Constitution gave women the right to vote. In 1948, Harry S. Truman issued an executive order integrating the US armed forces. In 1954, Brown versus the Board of Education of Topeka, Kansas declared racial segregation in schools to be unconstitutional.

In the 1960s, the Civil Rights movement led by Martin Luther King, Jr. erupted in America. It was a tumultuous period in American history that saw violent protests and the assassination of Dr. King. It ultimately resulted, however, in the passage of the Civil Rights Act, which prohibited discrimination based on race, colour, religion, or national origin, the implementation of affirmative action designed to create greater equality in higher education for minority students, and the beginning of African-American representation in Congress with the election of Shirley Chisholm as the first black female US representative. She went on to serve from 1969 to 1983. There have been numerous other notable accomplishments by African-Americans, including Guion Bluford Jr., who was the first African-American in space in 1983, Colin Powell, who was the first African-American Secretary of State in 2001, and Halle Berry, who was the first African-American woman to win the Best Actress Oscar for her role in *Monster's Ball*. Of course, no list of African-American accomplishments would be complete without including the election of President Barack Obama in 2008 as the first African-American president of the United States.

Despite these advances, there remain challenges. Far more African-Americans than the percentage they represent of the US population are incarcerated in US prisons and are subsequently denied the right to vote upon their release. Police killings of African-American suspected criminals far outnumber the killings of white suspected criminals. This has prompted recent protests, most notably the Black Lives Matter movement. Thus, the work that Harriet Tubman and many others like her began is not yet finished, but there is no doubt that the example she set continues to inspire those individuals of all races who struggle to ensure equality for all people. There is also no doubt she will continue to be an inspiration for many generations to come.

Conclusion

Harriet Tubman was born a slave and might have remained so had it not been for the circumstances that thrust greatness upon her. The confluence of events that helped form her personality and her moral compass gave her little choice but to pursue the actions she did in the struggle for freedom and equality. The final straw, as it were, was the Brodess family decision to sell her, which would have separated her from her family. She couldn't live with that any more than she could live with an uncertain future at the hands of slaveholders, so she made the decision to run away; with that decision, her life of service truly began.

Once free, Tubman realized that she had to help others achieve the same goal. She risked her own capture and likely death to guide others to the safety of the northern states. She dedicated herself fully to the cause of ending slavery in the United States. She lived a life of poverty, as any money she made she used to pay for helping others. She brought her family to freedom and countless others as well. She is credited with bringing over 300 slaves to freedom, and that doesn't even count her efforts to assist the Union army in bringing freedom to all slaves.

As a conductor on the Underground Railroad, Tubman's extensive knowledge of the southern terrain, particularly that of South Carolina and Maryland, provided invaluable assistance to the Union army, for which she acted as a guide and even led assaults. In each of these endeavors, she displayed extraordinary competence and valor. She did all of this despite lifelong consequences of an injury suffered in childhood that left her with a form of epilepsy, the symptoms of which included severe headaches and seizures, yet she soldiered on, quite literally. She worked as a nurse, personally witnessing the horrors of war, and she aided soldiers of all races as well as former slaves. Her compassion was unparalleled. She displayed uncommon bravery in the face of battles in which she participated. She was a valuable asset to the efforts of the Union army, and it is certain that her work contributed to the eventual victory of the north.

The end of the Civil War brought the changes she had hoped to see as all slaves were freed, yet that was not enough for her. She then took up the cause of women's suffrage. She worked tirelessly to secure the right of women to vote. She gave speeches and actively participated alongside notable suffragists to attain the goal of equality for all. Though she would not live to see it, her efforts paid off with the passage of the Nineteenth Amendment to the Constitution of the United States granting women the right to vote.

Aside from all the work she did assisting slaves and women in their quest for equality, she also dedicated herself to helping others. She supported her family members and took in people in need of help. She donated her money to the causes in which she believed, and as a result lived her life in poverty. She did so without receiving the recognition she so richly deserved for all that she did.

Her legacy lives on to this day. She has inspired generations of African-Americans as they have continued to struggle for their civil rights. She laid a foundation upon which they have been able to build their case for equality, and she did so in the most humble of ways, always crediting God with any success she had. Her faith gave her the courage to continue. She strongly believed that God would see her through and only take her when her work was done. Even as she struggled with her disability, she credited this to God as well, believing that it was his way of communicating with her and guiding her in her work.

While she could have lived a life pitying her condition as a slave, she instead used those experiences to build a moral base that would guide her actions into the future. Her insights can be seen in the quotes attributed to her in numerous biographies. They reveal the depth of her compassion and her thoughtful introspection regarding her life and her condition. She recognized the importance of liberty, comparing slavery to hell, but at the same time, she recognized that many slaveholders didn't know any better, saying at one point, "They acts up to the light they have." For this, she believed many of them would go to Heaven. She was truly an extraordinary woman and one of the most influential women in American history. Her actions have undeniably changed the world for the better. There is, perhaps, no better legacy than that and it is certain she will live on in the memories of those seeking freedom around the world.

Made in the
USA
Lexington, KY